FAMILIUS

DON'T WORRY BE HA

101 Deliciously Clever Food Puns

Marie Saba

Dedicated to John, Jack, and Elaine, with love. —M. S.

Copyright © 2021 by Marie Saba
All rights reserved.

Published by Familius LLC, www.familius.com
PO Box 1249, Reedley, CA 93654

Familius books are available at special discounts for bulk purchases, whether for sales promotions or
for family or corporate use. For more information, contact Familius Sales at orders@familius.com.

Library of Congress Control Number: 2021931732

Print ISBN 978-1-64170-464-9
Ebook ISBN 978-1-64170-511-0
KF 978-1-64170-531-8
FE 978-1-64170-551-6

Printed in China

Edited by Lindsay Sandberg
Cover and book design by Brooke Jorden

10 9 8 7 6 5 4 3 2 1

First Edition

Menu

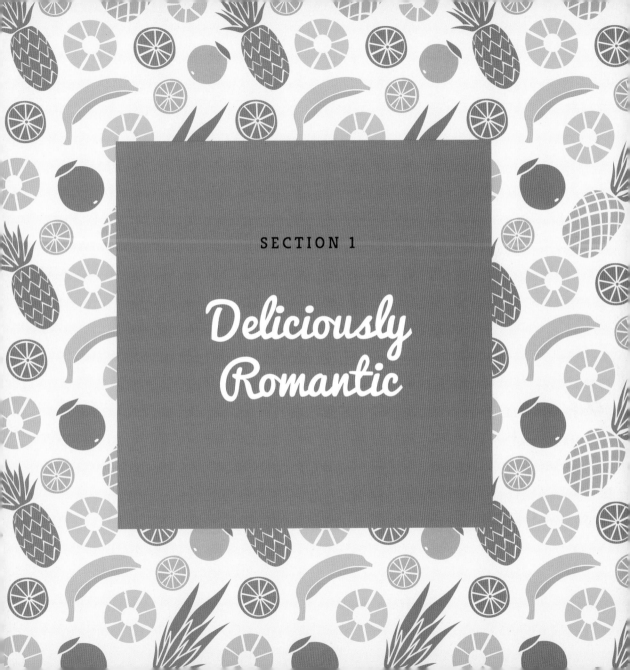

SECTION 1

Deliciously Romantic

I LOVE YOU A LOT

I'M ING FOR YOU

WE MAKE
A GREAT

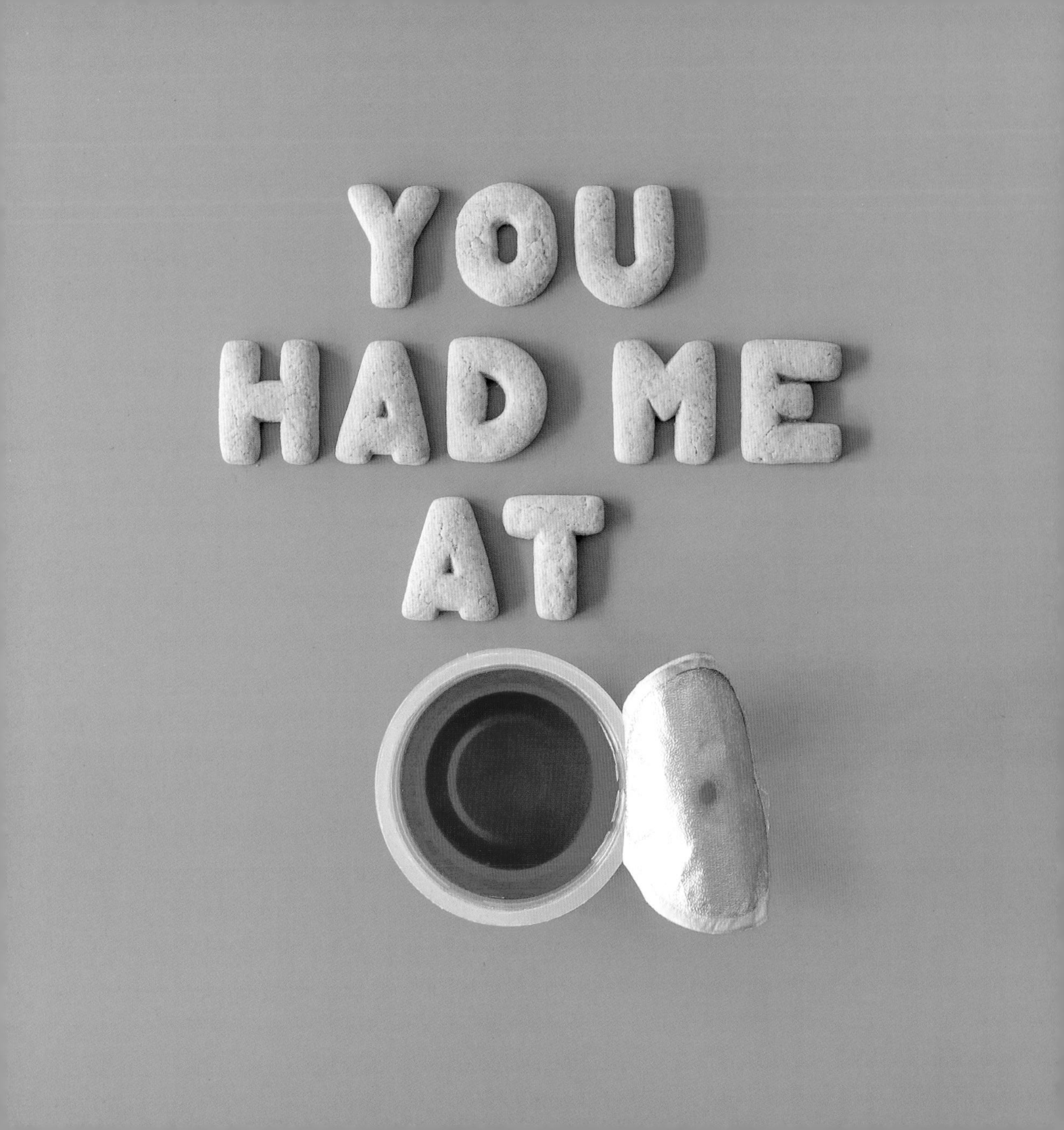
YOU
HAD ME
AT

YOU'RE
MY
====
HALF

YOU'RE THE

WE'RE
TO BE

SECTION 2

Movie Title Munchies

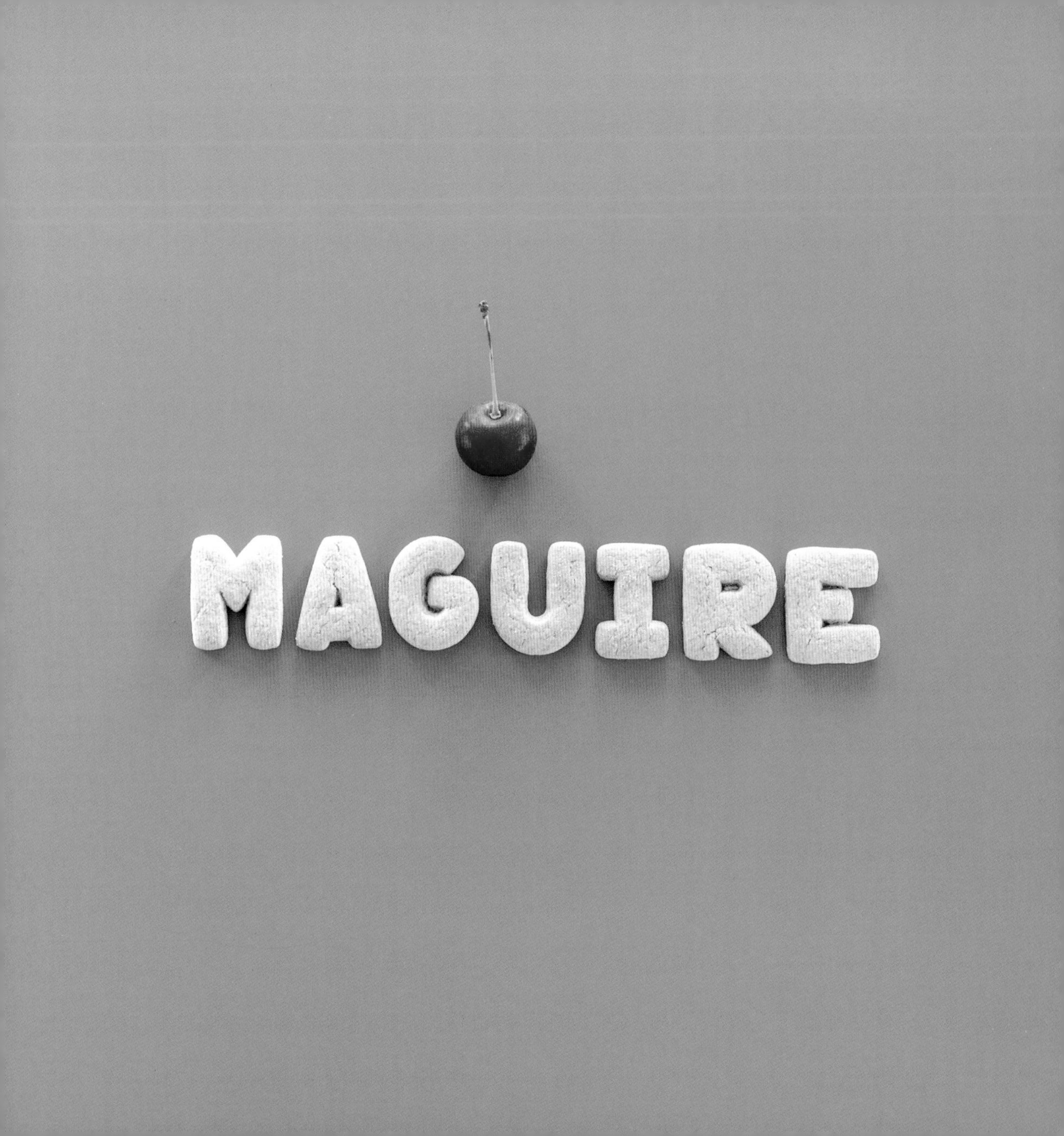
MAGUIRE

FICTION

PLANET OF THE

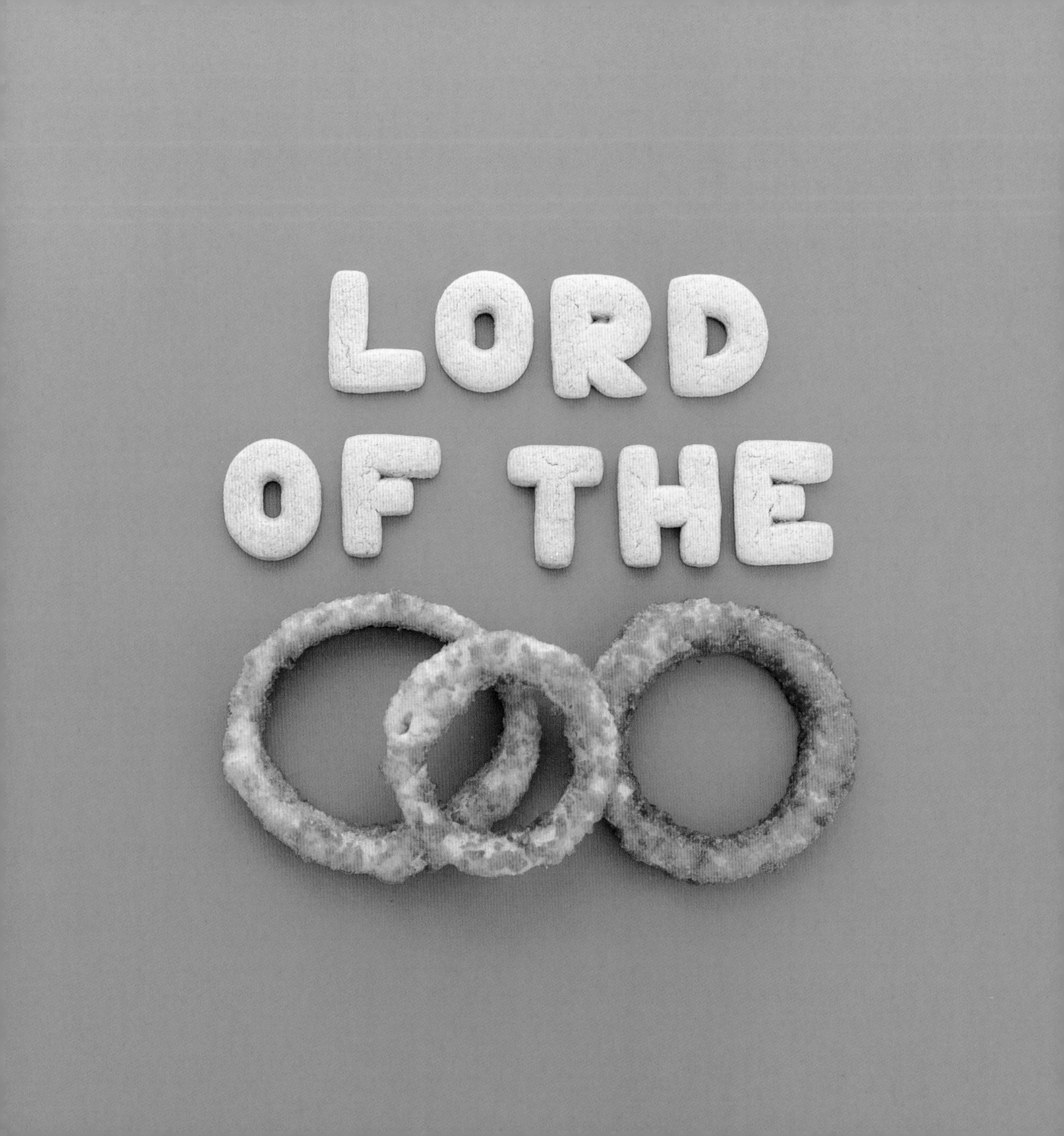
LORD
OF THE

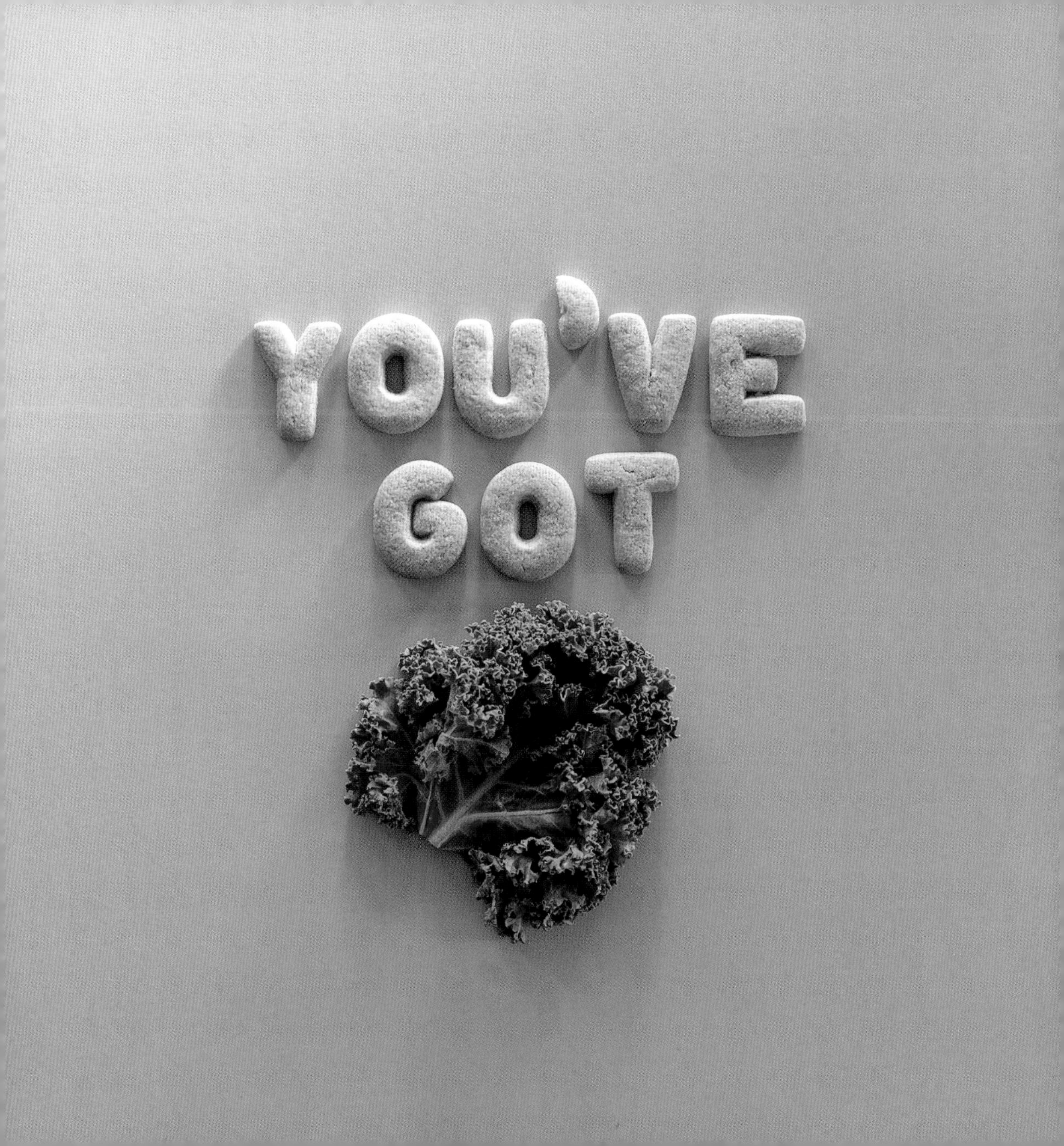
YOU'VE
GOT

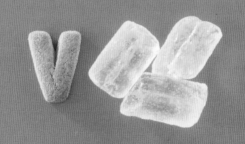

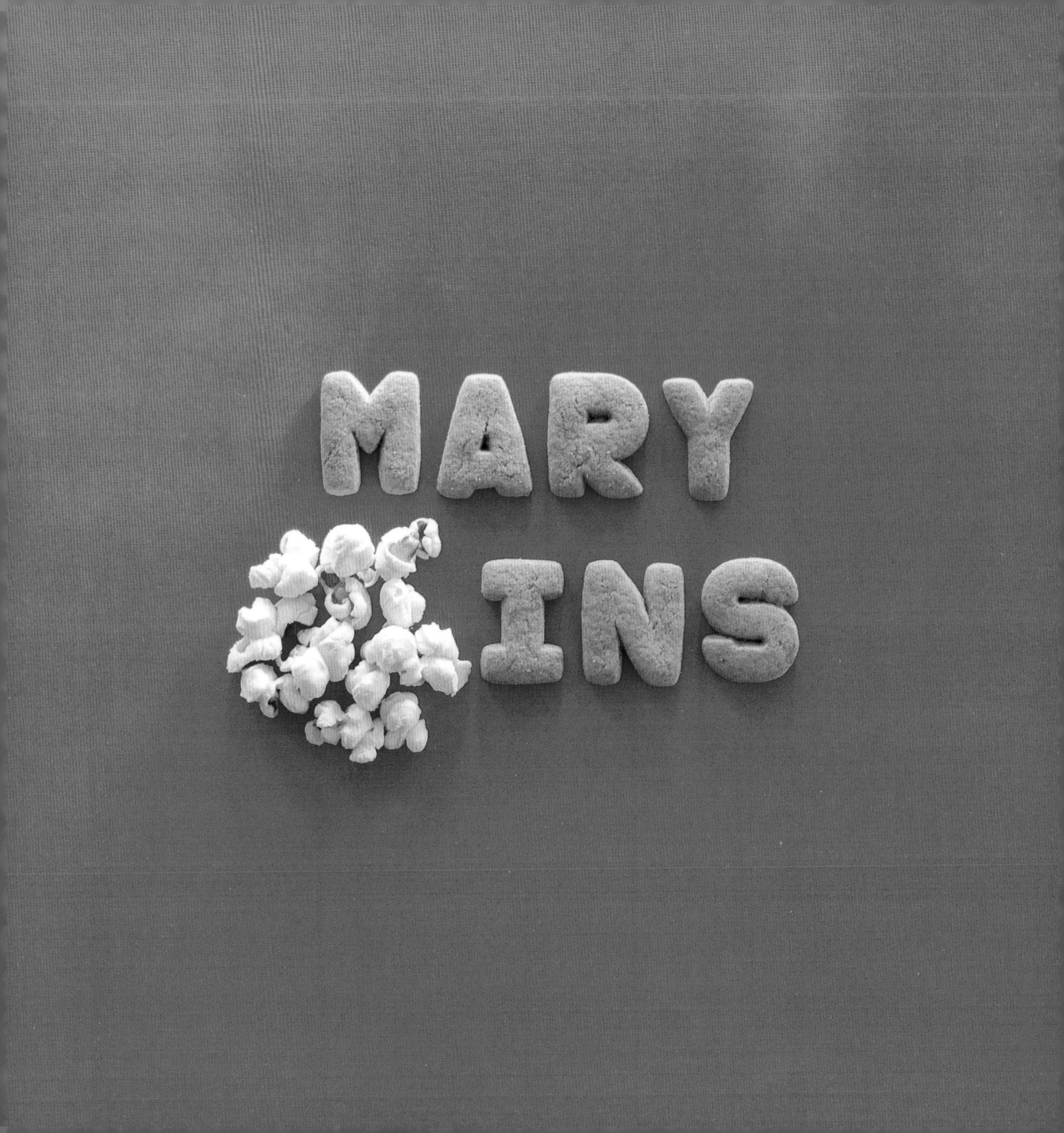
MARY
INS

FORREST
!P

SECTION 3

*Nom-Nom
Celeb Names*

ALYSSA

OLIVIA

JOHN

DANES

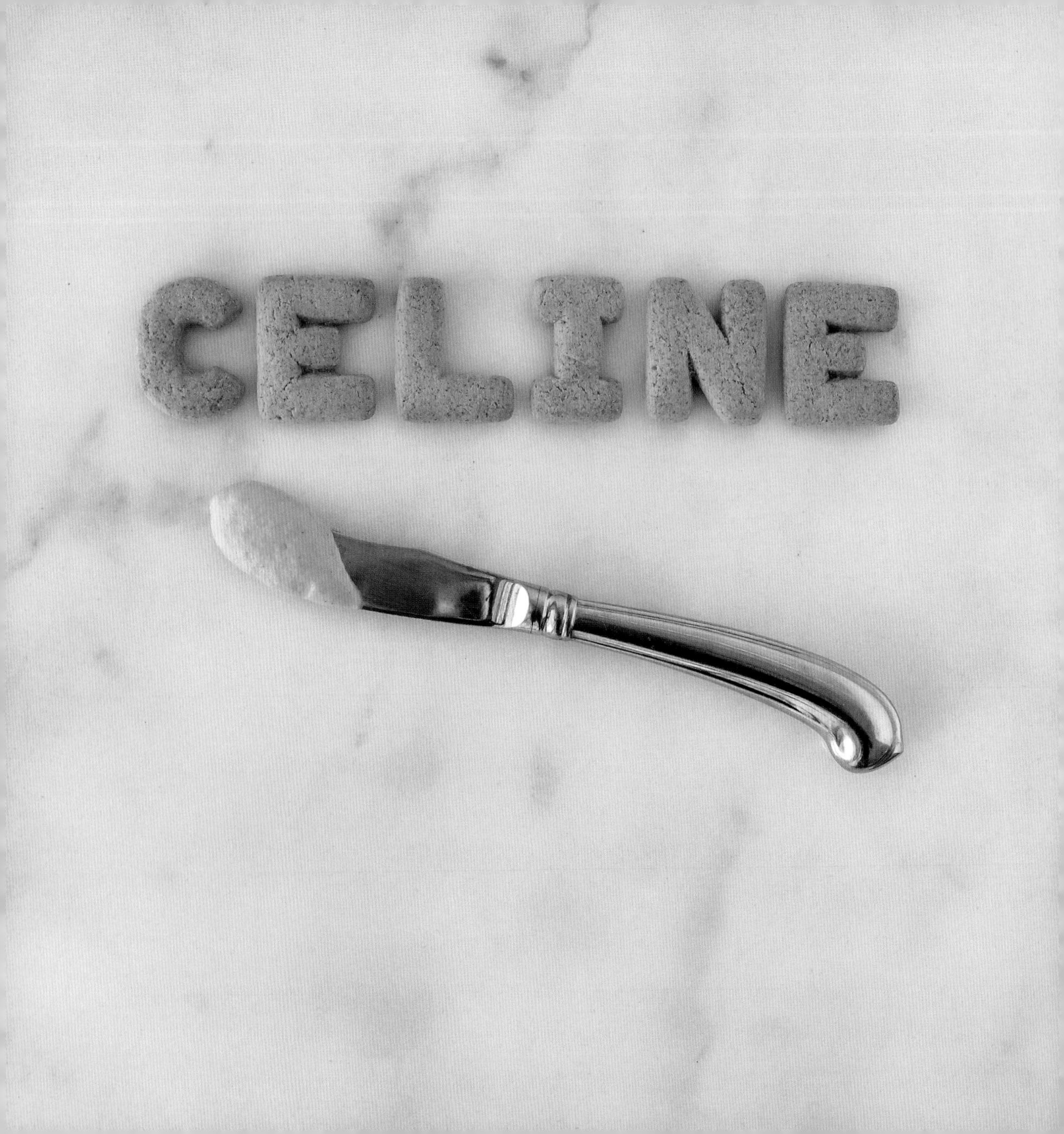
CELINE

ROBERT ■ JR.

DWIGHT OUM

HEATHER

DREW MORE

SECTION 4

Spicy Slang

EVERYDAY I'M ᴮᴿᵁˢˢᵉˡ IN'

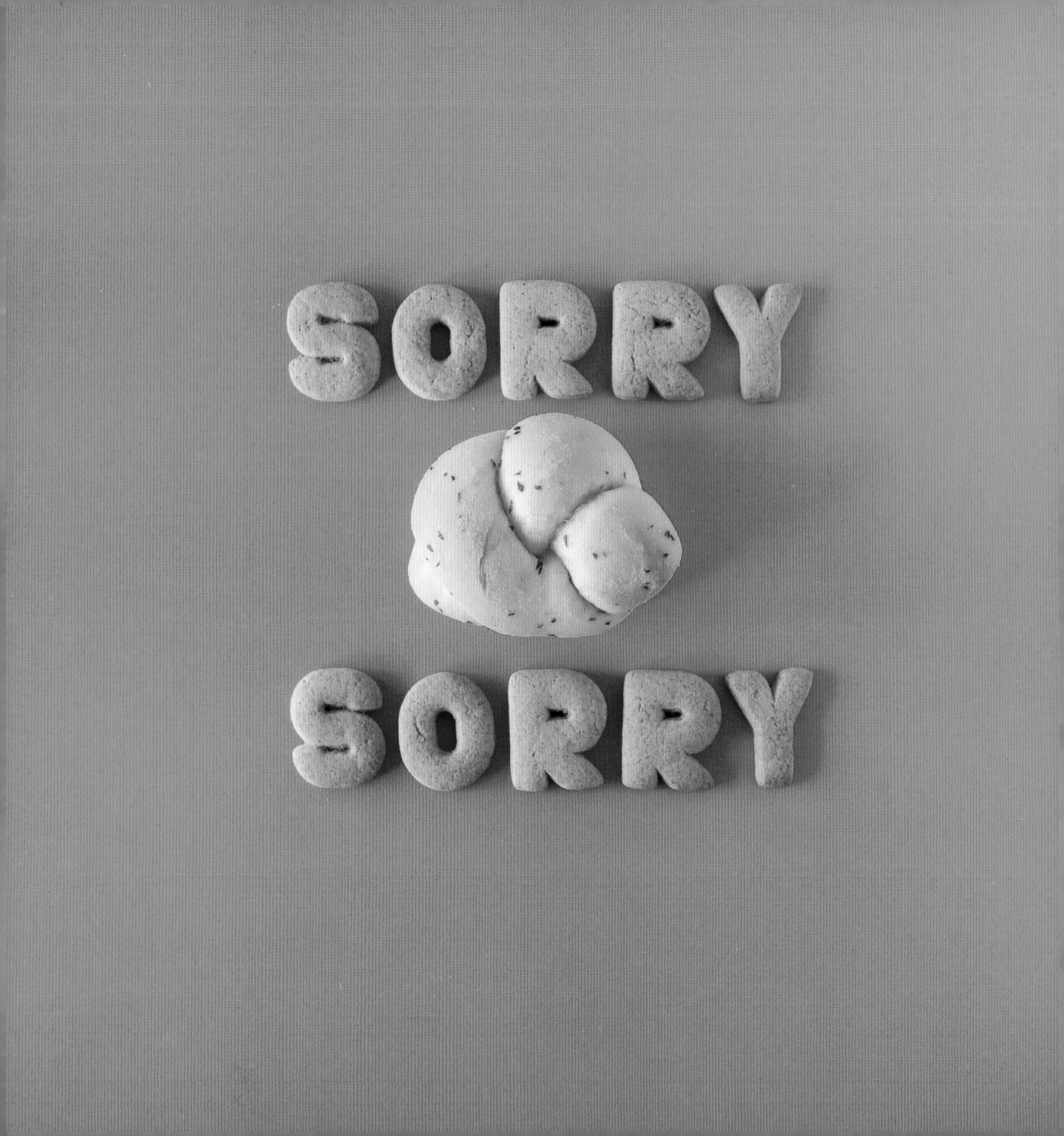
SORRY
SORRY

YOU'RE
SO
◯PE

YOU

MY

WORLD

SECTION 5

Sweet Inspiration

EVERY THING HAPPENS FOR A

DON'T WORRY BE HA

TRUST
THE
___ING
OF LIFE

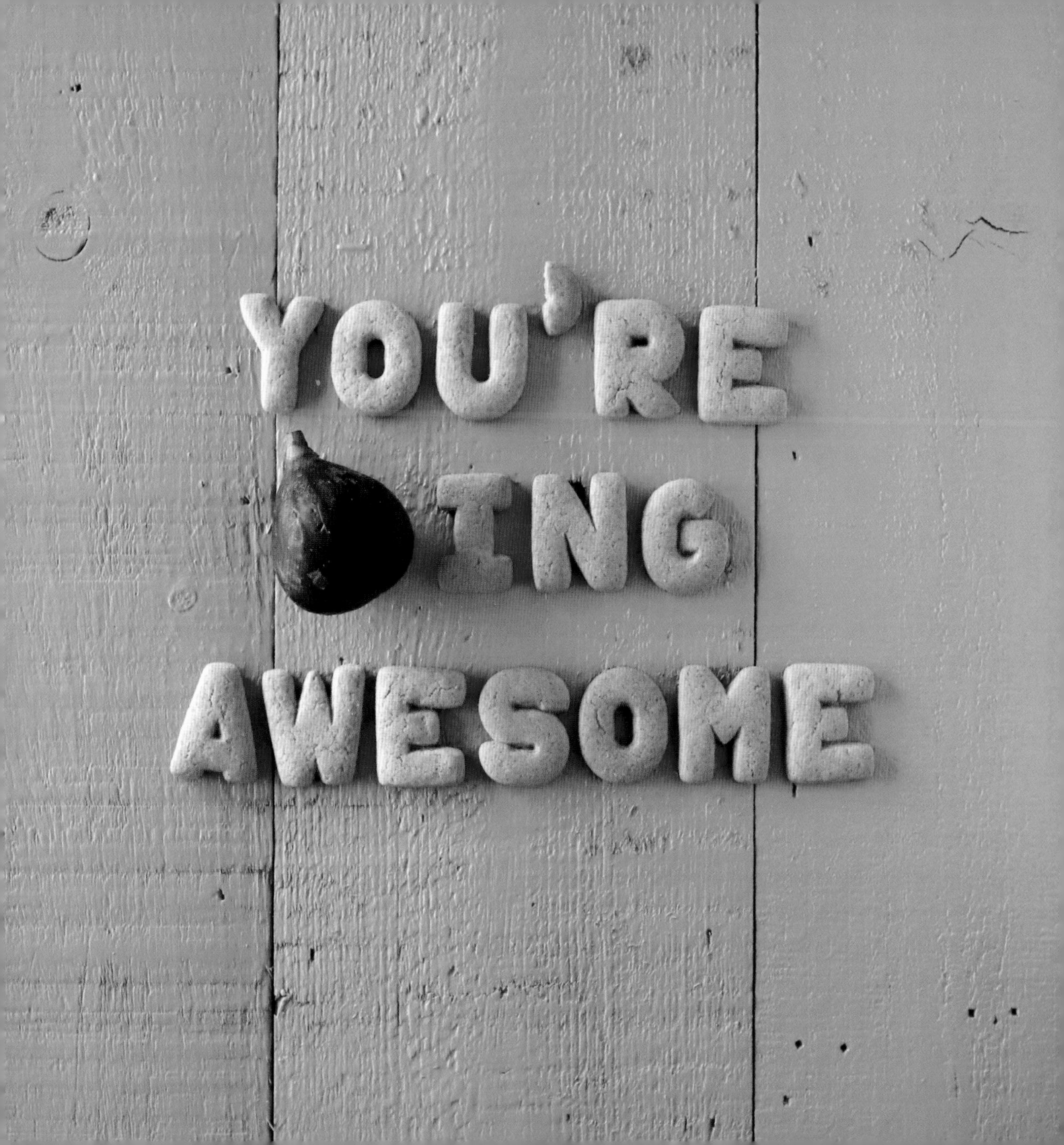
YOU'RE
ING
AWESOME

BRATE
YOUR
LIFE

BUT THE BEST

SECTION 6

Tasty Tourist Attractions

BUCKING PALACE/

MOUNT

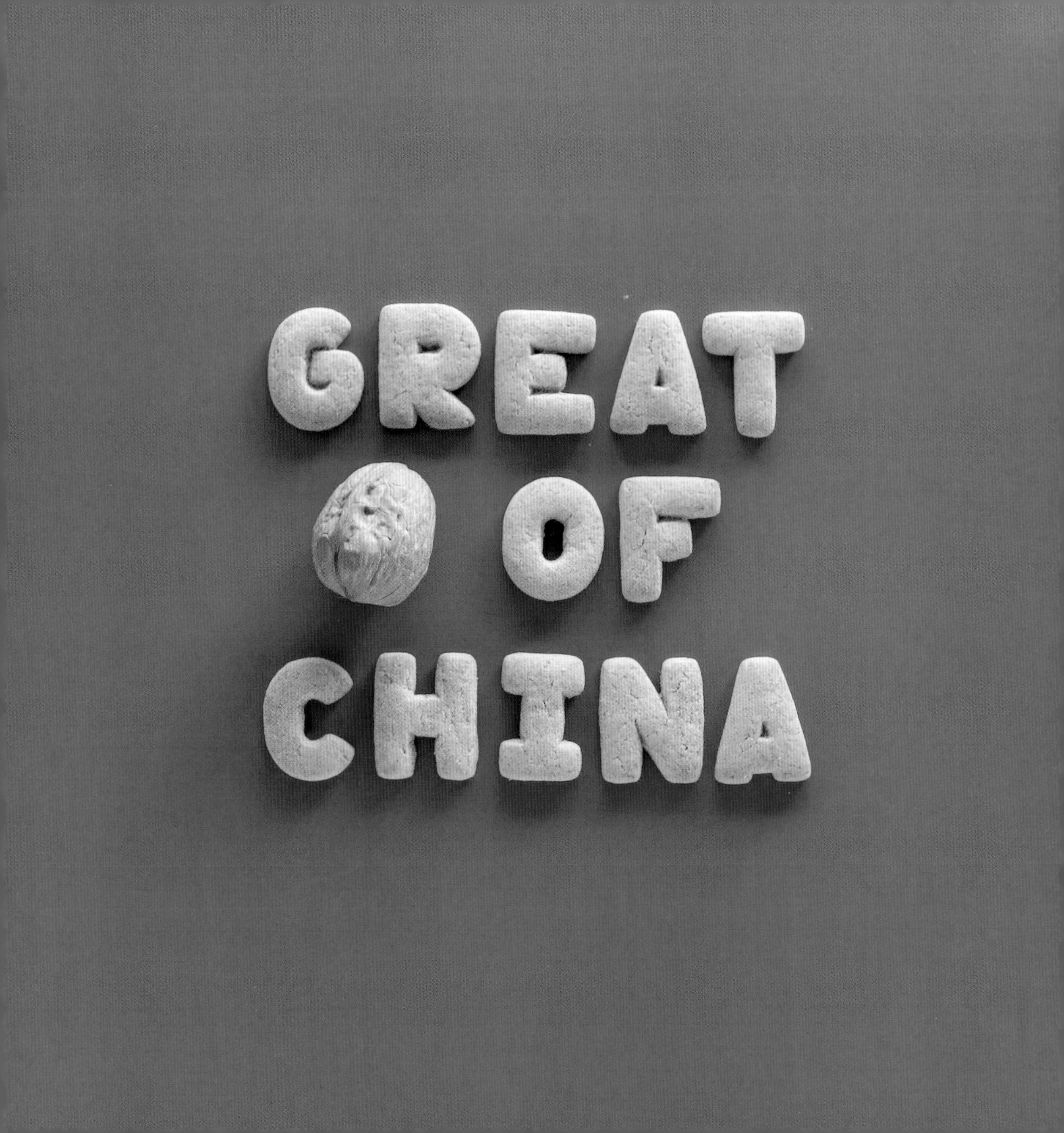
GREAT
OF
CHINA

EMPIRE

STATE

BUILDING

HENGE

SECTION 7

Yummy
Cartoon
Characters

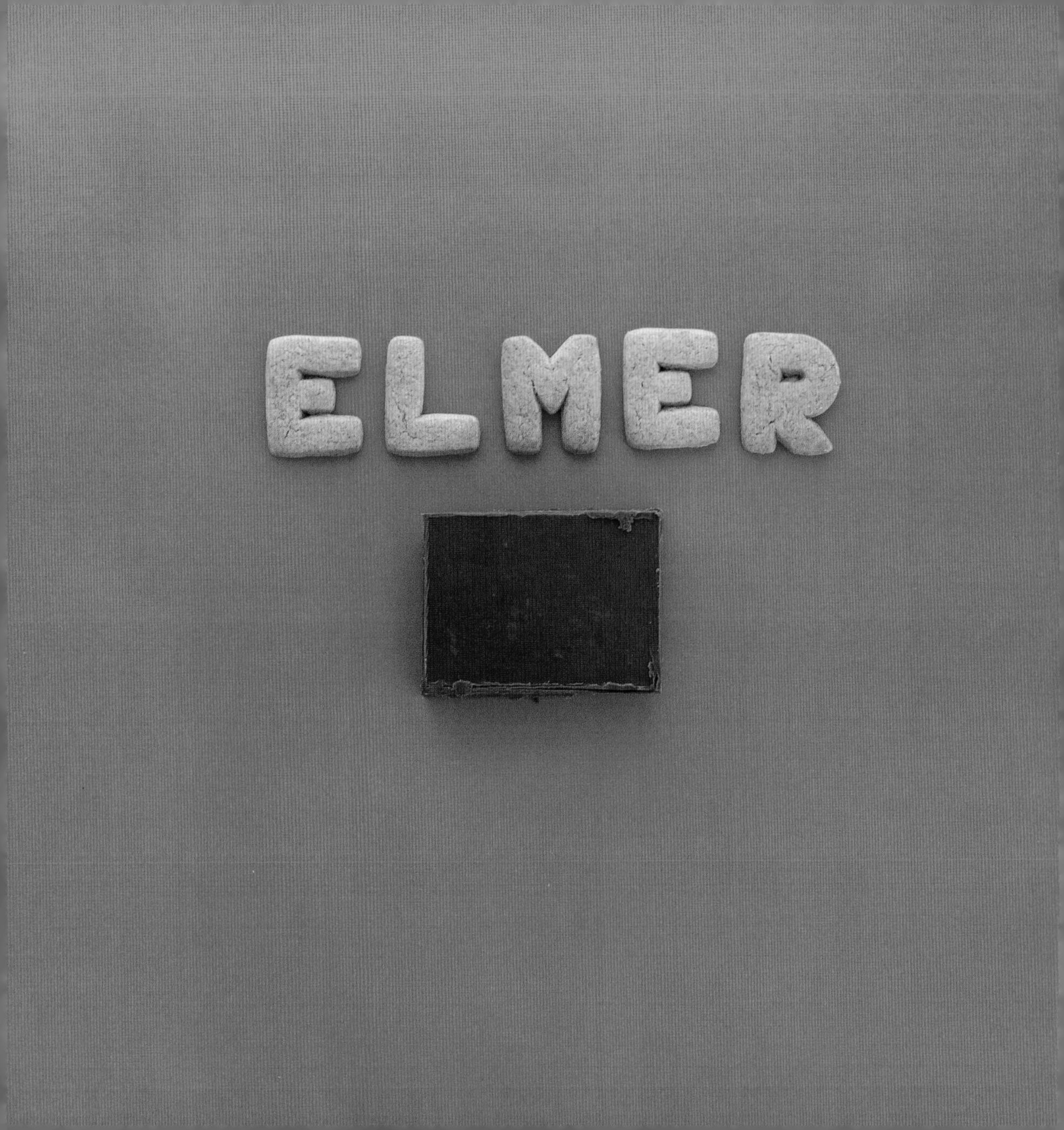
ELMER

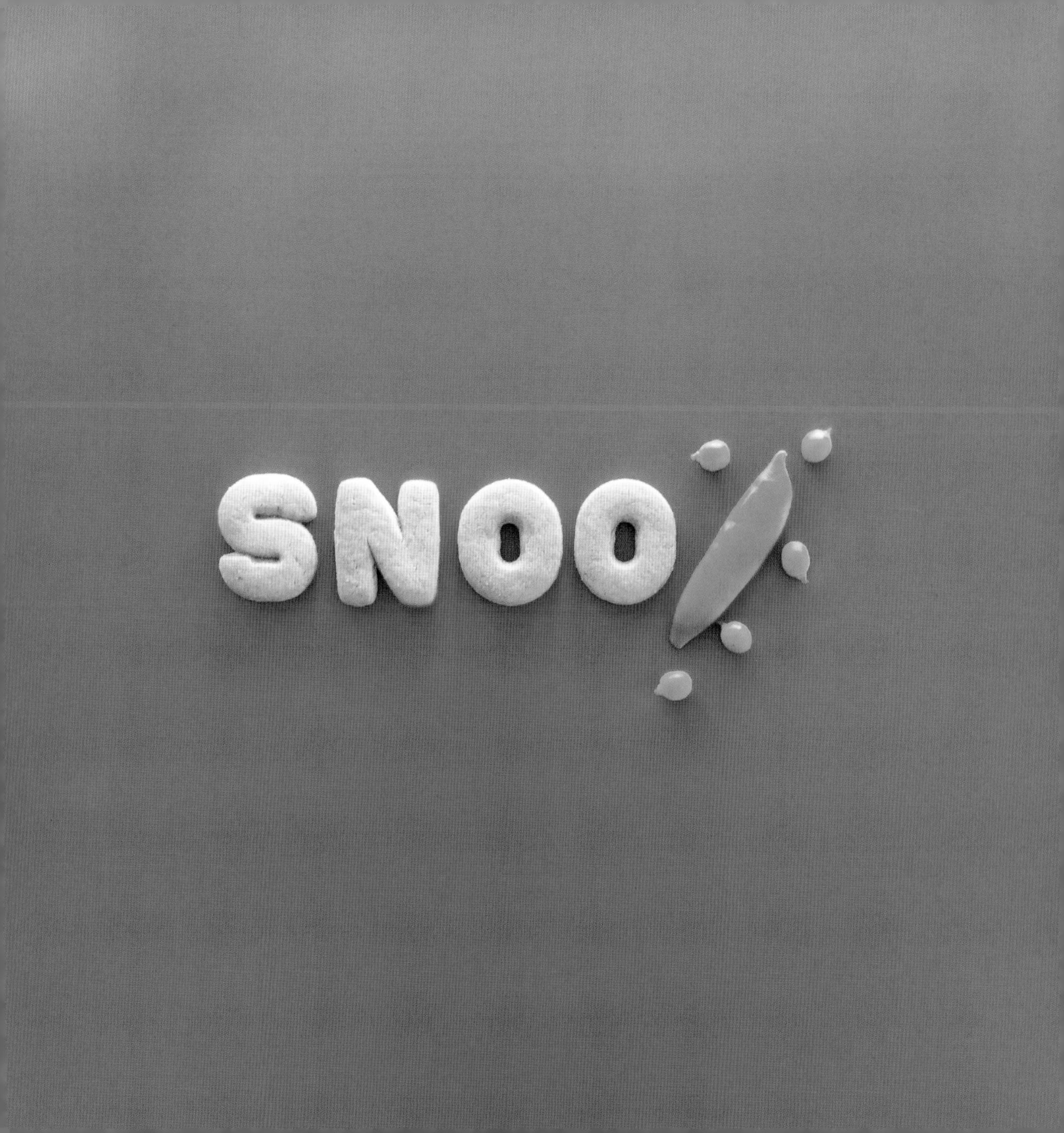
SNOO

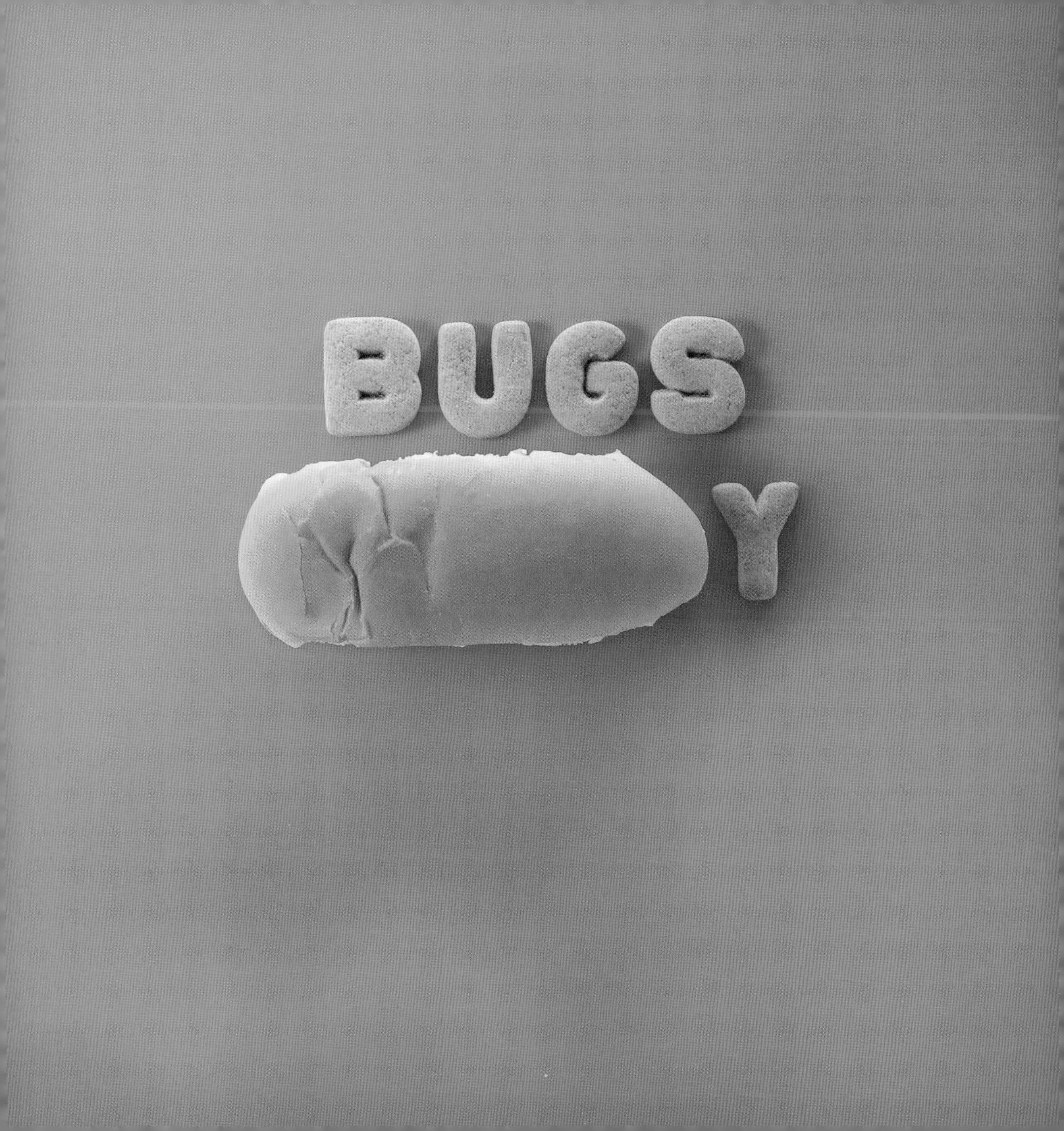
BUGS
Y

DUCK

PAN

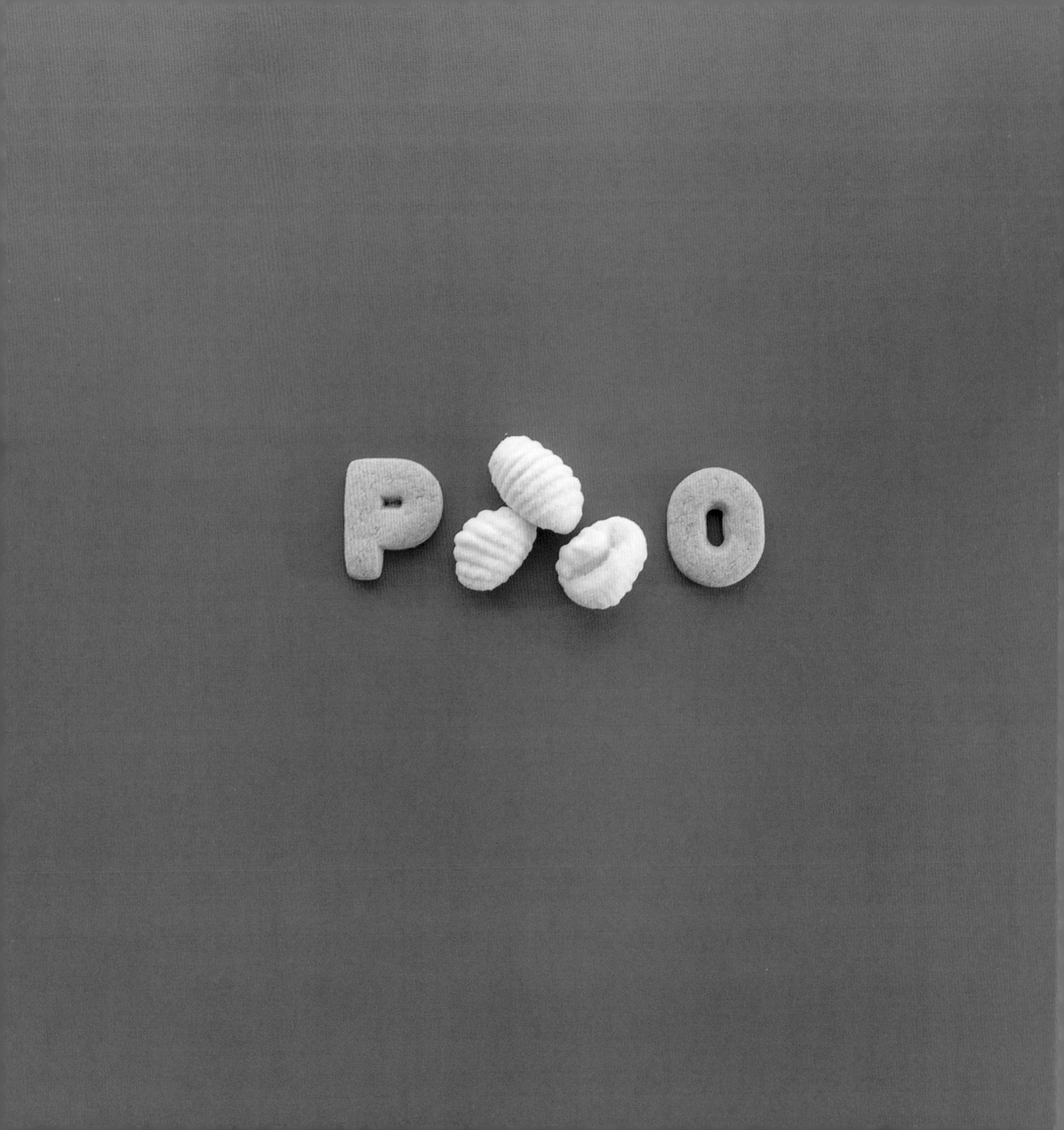

About the Author

Marie Saba, a former attorney, traded the courtroom for the kitchen in 2007 and never looked back. Now she's a stay-at-home mom and runs a popular Instagram account (@mariesaba), perhaps best known for its steady supply of quirky, creative, and inspirational food puns. Saba and her family live in Austin, Texas. You can visit her online at www.mariesaba.com.

THANKS A

About Familius

Visit Our Website: www.familius.com

Familius is a global trade publishing company that publishes books and other content to help families be happy. We believe that the family is the fundamental unit of society and that happy families are the foundation of a happy life. We recognize that every family looks different, and we passionately believe in helping all families find greater joy. To that end, we publish books for children and adults that invite families to live the Familius Ten Habits of Happy Family Life: *love together, play together, learn together, work together, talk together, heal together, read together, eat together, give together* and *laugh together*. Founded in 2012, Familius is located in Sanger, California.

Connect

Facebook: www.facebook.com/familiustalk
Twitter: @familiustalk, @paterfamilius1
Pinterest: www.pinterest.com/familius
Instagram: @familiustalk

FAMILIUS

The most important work you ever do will be within the walls of your own home.